Lessons from Roy

Written by **Kitty Dogwood**
Illustrated by **Kelly A. Fish**

Copyright © 2017 by GreatestFan Publishing
Text Copyright © 2017 by A.C. Gard
Illustrations Copyright © 2017 by Kelly A. Fish

All Rights Reserved. No part of this book may be reproduced or published in any form or by any means, or stored in a database retrieval system, without the prior written permission of the Publisher.

Published by GreatestFan Publishing, Durham, North Carolina
Book and cover design by Kelly A. Fish
Printed and bound in South Korea

Library of Congress Control Number: 2017950227
ISBN 978-0-9991453-0-2

10 9 8 7 6 5 4 3 2

Dedication

To Carolina fans ages 1 to 100.

We start this little story, below the Mason-Dixon line.
In the Old North State, where to take your time is fine.
Folks kind and polite, but that's just the start.
Doors opened for ladies, who're quick to "Bless Your Heart."

Sunday's reserved for church, Hallelujah, Praise the Lord.
Pull the car 'round after, of course, Chevy or Ford.
Barbeque and slaw for dinner, sweet tea at every meal.
Show respect for elders, give them love for real.

And in the mountains to the west, there lived a little boy.
A smart young man, whose Mamma named him Roy.

Like all little boys, he loved to play and run.
Play ball with his friends, have lots of fun.

And after playing ball, when craving something sweet,
He'd stop by Ed's, for a Coca-Cola treat.

And though cash was tight, Ole Roy's Mamma knew,
That to see her boy smile, she'd spare a dime or two.

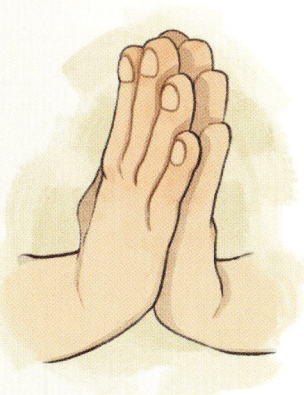  

These lessons he learned, as Mom's greatest fan,
He never forgot, as he grew to a man.
Say prayers, eat greens, do your chores every day.
Work hard, do your best, keep a smile come what may.

So off to school he went, a place close to home.
And he took to his school, like a dog to a bone.

And when it came time, to choose a career,
He knew right away, it was certainly clear.

"Coach basketball I will, that's my favorite sport.
Teach offense and defense, things of that sort.
Show kids how to dribble, pass, shoot, be a team.
Help others achieve and live out their dream."

Coaching came natural, cause that's what he knew.
And the more kids listened, the more that they grew.
Ole Roy had a knack, for making folks strong.
Helping boys become men, show right from wrong.

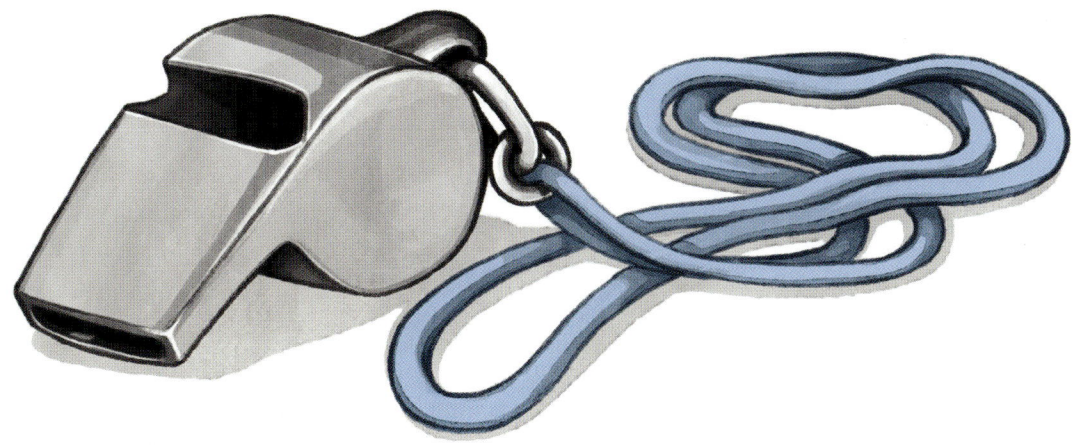

So he found a good job, in a town on a hill.
The perfect southern town, oh boy, what a thrill!
Where the people are nice, the sky Carolina Blue.
The perfect place to live and teach what he knew.

So he coached and he coached, teaching kids to play ball.
Teaching all whom he met, short kids and tall.
Kids of all colors, from the east and the west.
Welcomed all with a smile, put them all to the test.

Team players he wanted in every recruit,
To teach fundamentals, pass, dribble and shoot.
He'd teach the Four Corners, rebounding and more,
But emphasize the journey, far more than the score.

And much more important, than the skills of the sport,
Were the lessons he taught, that kids took from the court.
Show respect for others, give thanks for the pass,
Always play together, pay attention in class.

Dress nice, walk tall, keep a smile on your face.
Focus not on the prize, but the fun of the chase.

Please do your best, though you can't always win.
Be kind to all, ignore their color of skin.

And as the years passed, his teams won many games.
Players and teams became great, you know all the names.
Banners were hung, with great plays and dunks.
Roy coached 'em all, short shorts and baggy trunks.

But despite his success, he never forgot,
Friends who helped on the way to put him on top.

Wanda, Coach Smith, the best ever they say.

And Ole Buddy B, whom he chats with each day.

So whenever he's done, pray his lessons they stay.
Play hard, smart and together, it's the Carolina Way.
Have fun, study hard, be a good person each day.
And no matter what, respect all whom you play.

And when you're in town, stop by and check in.
Come cheer on the Heels, check to see how they've been.
Roy'll save a time-out, just for you, yes he will.
Until then, all the best, from the town on the hill.

Meet the author, Kitty Dogwood

Favorite Song: Carolina in My Mind

Favorite Color: Carolina Blue

Favorite Food: BBQ, slaw and hush puppies

3 Tar Heels from History she'd have dinner with: Dean Smith, Mia Hamm, Michael Jordan

Favorite Tar Heels moment in history: Any time Carolina beats dook

Kitty's Pets: Bulldog named Franklin, guinea pig named Rosemary

Glossary

Page 4
Often thought of as the dividing line between the northern and southern states, the Mason-Dixon line was surveyed between 1763 and 1767 by Charles Mason and Jeremiah Dixon to resolve a border dispute between Maryland, Pennsylvania and Delaware.

"The Old North State" is the official state song of North Carolina, written by William Gaston in 1835.

Page 7
Ford Motor Company (Ford) was founded in 1903 by Henry Ford, and Chevrolet (Chevy) was founded in 1911 by Louis Chevrolet and William Durant. From the beginning, Ford and Chevy have been rival automobile manufacturers. The rivalry has particular significance in North Carolina, the home of the National Association for Stock Car Auto Racing (NASCAR). NASCAR can trace its origins to bootlegging during Prohibition, when drivers ran whiskey throughout the Appalachian Mountains. The NASCAR Hall of Fame is in Charlotte, NC.

Page 8
Roy was born in the Appalachian Mountains and grew up predominantly in Asheville, NC. He attended Biltmore Elementary School and T.C. Roberson High School.

Page 10-11
As a boy, Roy and his friends frequented Ed's service station to quench their thirst with Coca-Colas after playing basketball. When Roy's Mom, known as Mimmie to her friends, discovered that Roy didn't have the 10 cents to buy himself a Coke, she started leaving him a dime on the kitchen counter even though times were tight, a gesture Roy never forgot.

Page 13
For most of Roy's life, Mimmie was a single Mom raising Roy and his sister Frances. She was a loving mother and often worked multiple jobs to provide for her family.

Glossary

Page 14-15
Roy attended The University of North Carolina at Chapel Hill (UNC) from 1968 to 1972 and played two years on the UNC Junior Varsity basketball team. As a sophomore, he attended varsity basketball practices and learned from Hall of Fame coach Dean Smith.

Page 20
Roy coached at Charles D. Owens High School in Black Mountain, NC, from 1973 to 1978. From 1978 to 1988 he was an assistant coach at UNC under Dean Smith before serving as the Kansas Jayhawks head coach from 1988 to 2003. Roy returned to UNC in 2003 as head coach and led UNC to NCAA Championships in 2005, 2009 and 2017.

Page 24
In the 1960s Dean Smith ran the Four Corners offense at UNC. It's an offense in which four players stand in the corners of the court, and the fifth player handles the ball in the middle. The goal is to play "keep away" from the opponent and run down the clock. The offense was so effective that it led to the institution of the shot clock rule. On February 21, 2015 in Chapel Hill, Roy honored Coach Smith by running the Four Corners against Georgia Tech. Coach Smith passed away on February 7, 2015.

Page 27
Dean Smith is credited with several basketball innovations that are commonplace in the sport today. He was a proponent of the dunk when it was outlawed from 1967 to 1976. He made his players point to the passer to thank them for an assist, and he made bench players stand and cheer their teammates after successful plays and when leaving the court. He's even been credited with the team huddle teams use before free throws to take advantage of the stoppage in play.

Glossary

Page 32
Roy met his wife Wanda when they were both students at UNC. They married in 1973 and have two children, Scott and Kimberly. Buddy Baldwin was Roy's basketball coach at T.C. Roberson High School and one of the biggest influences in his life.

Page 33
The Carolina Way is UNC's philosophy for how to live one's life in a positive way, both on and off the court. "Play hard, play smart, play together."

Page 35
Like his mentor Coach Smith, Roy believes in saving time-outs for the end of games. He often won't call time-outs so the opponent can't set up its defense. Roy's philosophy tested positive on March 26, 2017 against the Kentucky Wildcats. With seven seconds left in the 2017 NCAA Tournament, Kentucky's Malik Monk made a 3-pointer to tie the game in the Elite Eight in Memphis, TN. Rather than calling a time-out after the made basket, UNC inbounded immediately, pushing the ball down the court, not allowing Kentucky to set its defense. In the confusion, Theo Pinson passed to Luke Maye who drained a 2-pointer with 0.3 seconds remaining. UNC won the game and went on to win the 2017 NCAA Championship.